This Anxiety Bullet Journal *(with mindfulness prompts)*

BELONGS TO:

_____

DEDICATION

This Ultimate Anxiety Mindfulness Bullet Notebook is dedicated to all the anxious types out there who love to plan out calming exercises, and document their findings in the process.

You are my inspiration for producing books and I'm honored to be a part of keeping all of your notes and records organized.

How to use this Anxiety Bullet Journal Notebook:

This useful anxiety and mindfulness log book is a must-have for anyone that loves to write out their anxious thoughts and work on a better self care routine! You will love this easy to use journal to track and record all your self care activities.

Each interior page includes space to record & track the following:

Anxiety Worksheet - Write down how you reacted to an incident.
Anxiety Tracker - Use this graph to track how you are doing.
Mood Tracker - Color in the circle or vertical mood tracker.
Nighttime Worries - Fill in the space with night time worries.
Mindfulness Worksheets Include:
Safe Space - Record your thoughts and sketches here.
Body Scan - Track and write down your body scan results and sensations.
Finger Labyrinth - Trace your finger on the path.
Grounding Yourself - Visualize and redirect your thoughts here.
Happy Memory Clouds - Use them when emotions become overwhelming.

If you are new to the world of anxiety or have been at it for a while, this ultimate anxiety workbook organizer is a must have! Can make a great useful gift for anyone that needs a daily calm!

Bless!

A Safe Space

Title of space _____

Sketch your safe space here

Words that describe your space

Sounds

Sights

Smells

Textures

People and animals present

A Safe Space

Title of space _____

Sketch your safe space here

Words that describe your space

Sounds

Sights

Smells

Textures

People and animals present

A Safe Space

Title of space _____

Sketch your safe space here

Words that describe your space

Sounds

Sights

Smells

Textures

People and animals present

A Safe Space

Title of space _____

Sketch your safe space here

Words that describe your space

Sounds

Sights

Smells

Textures

People and animals present

A Safe Space

Title of space _____

Sketch your safe space here

Words that describe your space

Sounds

Sights

Smells

Textures

People and animals present

Body Scan

Today's Date _____   Time _____

Where are you? _____

Head and Face

Neck and Shoulders

Spine

Hips and Pelvis

Chest

Stomach

Arms

Legs

Whole body sensations

Sensations

Warm - Cold - Soft - Hard - Breeze - Damp - Dry

Tense - Strong - Taut - Numb - Tingling - Tickling - Muscle - Slender - Fragile

Pressure - Throbbing - Blocked - Pulse - Stabbing - Quivering

Nauseous - Shaking - Aching - Breathless - Wired - Anxious

Soothed - Relaxed - Comfortable - Free Flowing

Body Scan

Today's Date _____ Time _____

Where are you? _____

Head and Face

Neck and Shoulders

Spine

Hips and Pelvis

Chest

Stomach

Arms

Legs

Whole body sensations

Sensations

Warm - Cold - Soft - Hard - Breeze - Damp - Dry

Tense - Strong - Taut - Numb - Tingling - Tickling - Muscle - Slender - Fragile

Pressure - Throbbing - Blocked - Pulse - Stabbing - Quivering

Nauseous - Shaking - Aching - Breathless - Wired - Anxious

Soothed - Relaxed - Comfortable - Free Flowing

Body Scan

Today's Date _____   Time _____

Where are you? _____

Head and Face

Neck and Shoulders

Spine

Hips and Pelvis

Chest

Stomach

Arms

Legs

Whole body sensations

Sensations

Warm - Cold - Soft - Hard - Breeze - Damp - Dry

Tense - Strong - Taut - Numb - Tingling - Tickling - Muscle - Slender - Fragile

Pressure - Throbbing - Blocked - Pulse - Stabbing - Quivering

Nauseous - Shaking - Aching - Breathless - Wired - Anxious

Soothed - Relaxed - Comfortable - Free Flowing

Body Scan

Today's Date _____   Time _____

Where are you? _____

Head and Face

Neck and Shoulders

Spine

Hips and Pelvis

Chest

Stomach

Arms

Legs

Whole body sensations

Sensations

Warm - Cold - Soft - Hard - Breeze - Damp - Dry

Tense - Strong - Taut - Numb - Tingling - Tickling - Muscle - Slender - Fragile

Pressure - Throbbing - Blocked - Pulse - Stabbing - Quivering

Nauseous - Shaking - Aching - Breathless - Wired - Anxious

Soothed - Relaxed - Comfortable - Free Flowing

Body Scan

Today's Date _____   Time _____

Where are you? _____

Head and Face

Neck and Shoulders

Spine

Hips and Pelvis

Chest

Stomach

Arms

Legs

Whole body sensations

Sensations

Warm - Cold - Soft - Hard - Breeze - Damp - Dry

Tense - Strong - Taut - Numb - Tingling - Tickling - Muscle - Slender - Fragile

Pressure - Throbbing - Blocked - Pulse - Stabbing - Quivering

Nauseous - Shaking - Aching - Breathless - Wired - Anxious

Soothed - Relaxed - Comfortable - Free Flowing

Finger Labyrinth

Use your finger to slowly trace a path to the center of the labyrinth

Breathe calmly and slowly as you focus.
When you reach the center, draw a long deep breath or two.

Then trace your path back to the outside
Repeat until you feel more focused and calm.

Focus Words

Breathe - Peace - Relax - Tranquility - Serenity - Calm - Space - Beauty
Love - Wonder - Kindness - Light - Happiness - Joy - Warmth

Observations

Finger Labyrinth

Use your finger to slowly trace a path to the center of the labyrinth

Breathe calmly and slowly as you focus.
When you reach the center, draw a long deep breath or two.

Then trace your path back to the outside
Repeat until you feel more focused and calm.

Focus Words

Breathe - Peace - Relax - Tranquility - Serenity - Calm - Space - Beauty
Love - Wonder - Kindness - Light - Happiness - Joy - Warmth

Observations

Finger Labyrinth

Use your finger to slowly trace a path to the center of the labyrinth

Breathe calmly and slowly as you focus.
When you reach the center, draw a long deep breath or two.

Then trace your path back to the outside
Repeat until you feel more focused and calm.

Focus Words

Breathe - Peace - Relax - Tranquility - Serenity - Calm - Space - Beauty
Love - Wonder - Kindness - Light - Happiness - Joy - Warmth

Observations

Finger Labyrinth

Use your finger to slowly trace a path to the center of the labyrinth

Breathe calmly and slowly as you focus.
When you reach the center, draw a long deep breath or two.

Then trace your path back to the outside
Repeat until you feel more focused and calm.

Focus Words

Breathe - Peace - Relax - Tranquility - Serenity - Calm - Space - Beauty
Love - Wonder - Kindness - Light - Happiness - Joy - Warmth

Observations

Finger Labyrinth

Use your finger to slowly trace a path to the center of the labyrinth

Breathe calmly and slowly as you focus.
When you reach the center, draw a long deep breath or two.

Then trace your path back to the outside
Repeat until you feel more focused and calm.

Focus Words

Breathe - Peace - Relax - Tranquility - Serenity - Calm - Space - Beauty
Love - Wonder - Kindness - Light - Happiness - Joy - Warmth

Observations

Grounding Yourself

Today's Date _____

What is your name? _____

Where are you?

[ ]

Words that describe your space

[ ]

Who is with you? What are they doing?

[ ]

Words that describe your feelings

[ ]

What do you hear?

[ ]

What do you see?

[ ]

What can you smell?

[ ]

What can you touch?

[ ]

When you are calm, set an intention:

[ ]

Grounding Yourself

Today's Date _____

What is your name? _____

Where are you?

Words that describe your space

Who is with you? What are they doing?

Words that describe your feelings

What do you hear?

What do you see?

What can you smell?

What can you touch?

When you are calm, set an intention:

Grounding Yourself

Today's Date _____

What is your name? _____

Where are you?

Words that describe your space

Who is with you? What are they doing?

Words that describe your feelings

What do you hear?

What do you see?

What can you smell?

What can you touch?

When you are calm, set an intention:

Grounding Yourself

Today's Date _____

What is your name? _____

Where are you?

Words that describe your space

Who is with you? What are they doing?

Words that describe your feelings

What do you hear?

What do you see?

What can you smell?

What can you touch?

When you are calm, set an intention:

Grounding Yourself

Today's Date _____

What is your name? _____

Where are you?

Words that describe your space

Who is with you? What are they doing?

Words that describe your feelings

What do you hear?

What do you see?

What can you smell?

What can you touch?

When you are calm, set an intention:

Happy Memory Clouds

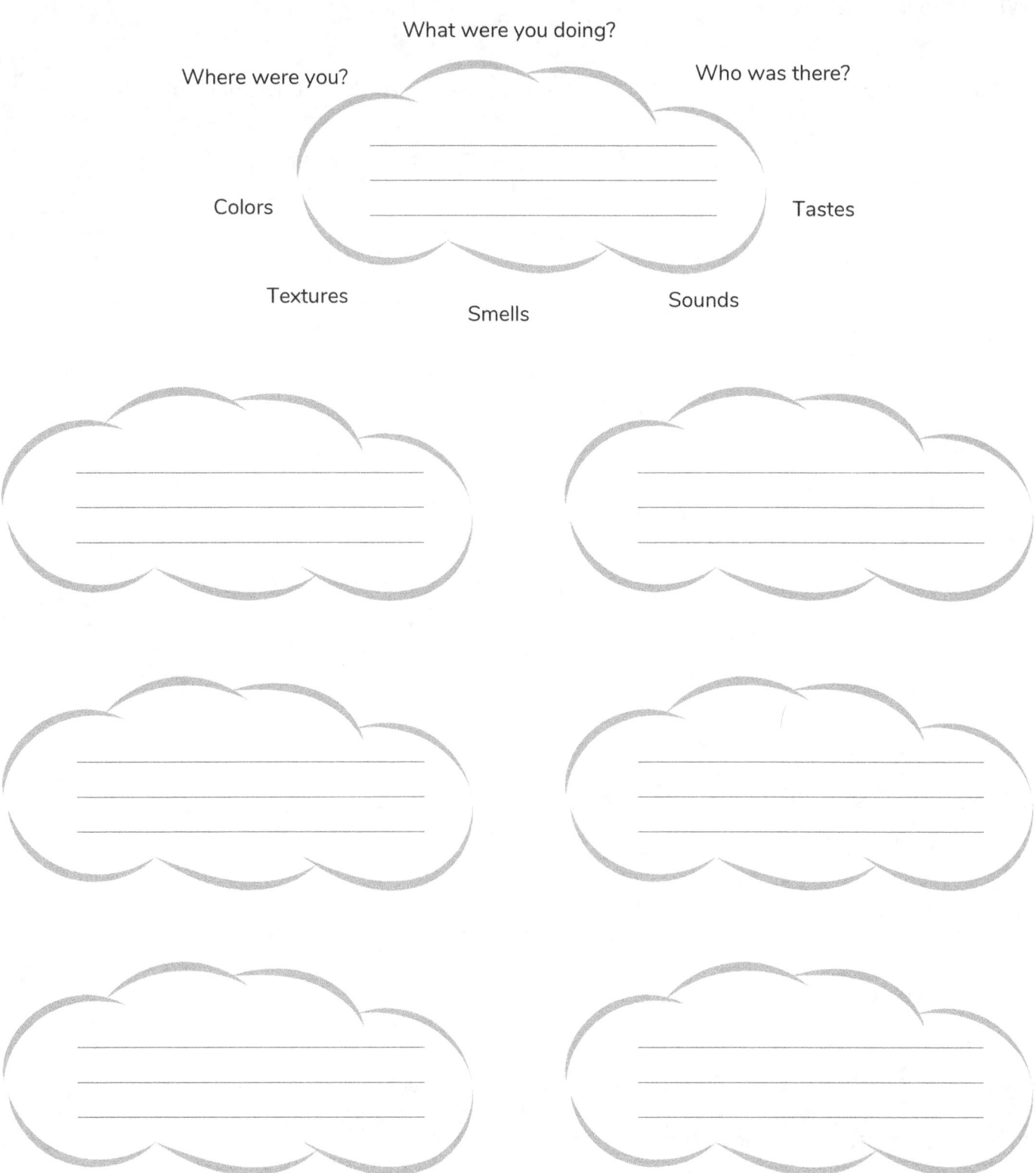

Where were you?   What were you doing?   Who was there?

Colors   Tastes

Textures   Smells   Sounds

Fill out these clouds as you think of happy memories.
Use them when your emotions become overwhelming.

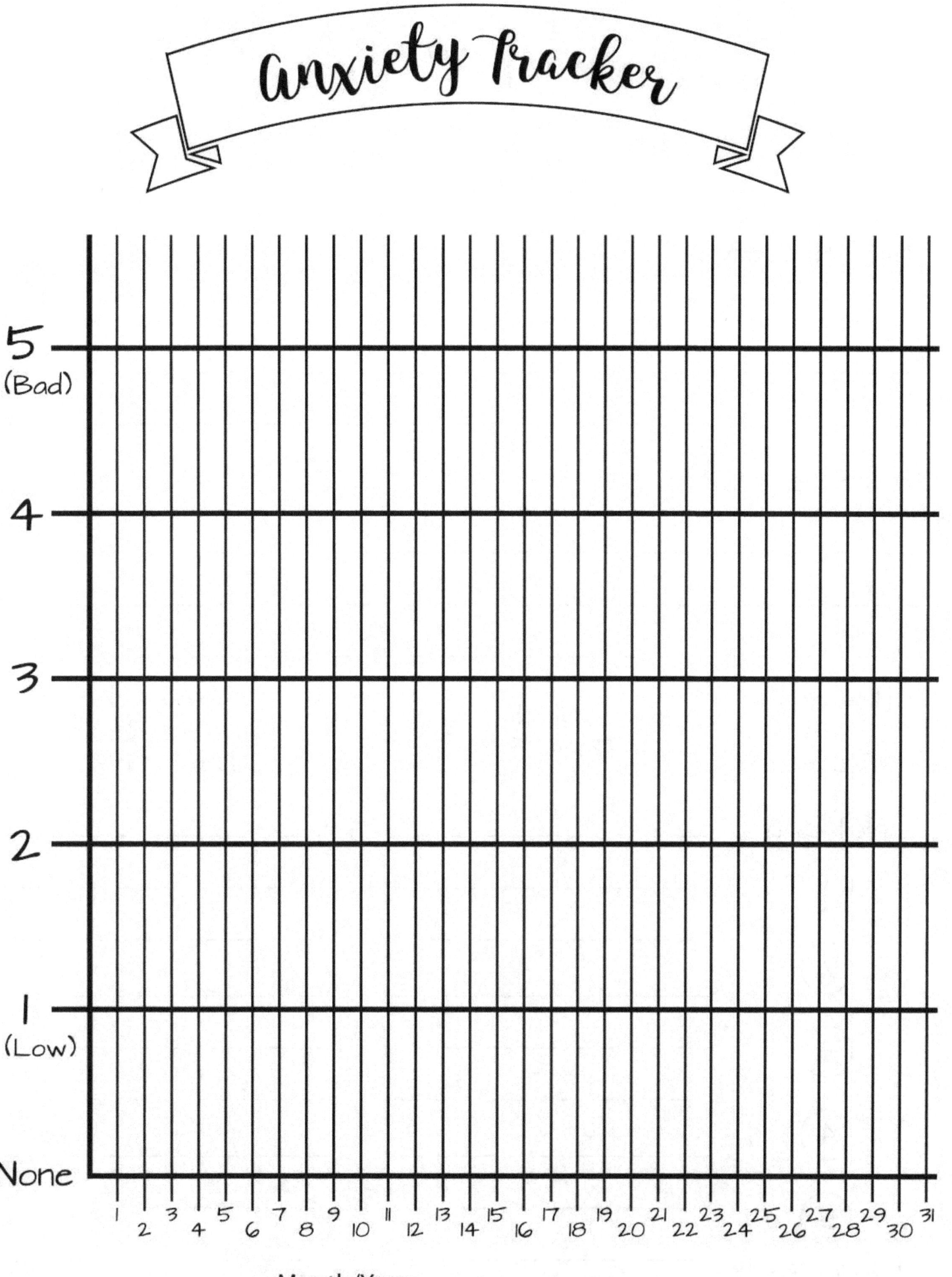

Date: _____

What Happened
_____
_____
_____

How I Reacted
_____
_____
_____

How Bad is it Really?	What I Think/Feel	How I'd Like to React Next Time
Not Bad	_____	_____
①	_____	_____
②	_____	_____
③	_____	_____
④	_____	_____
⑤	_____	_____
Really Bad		

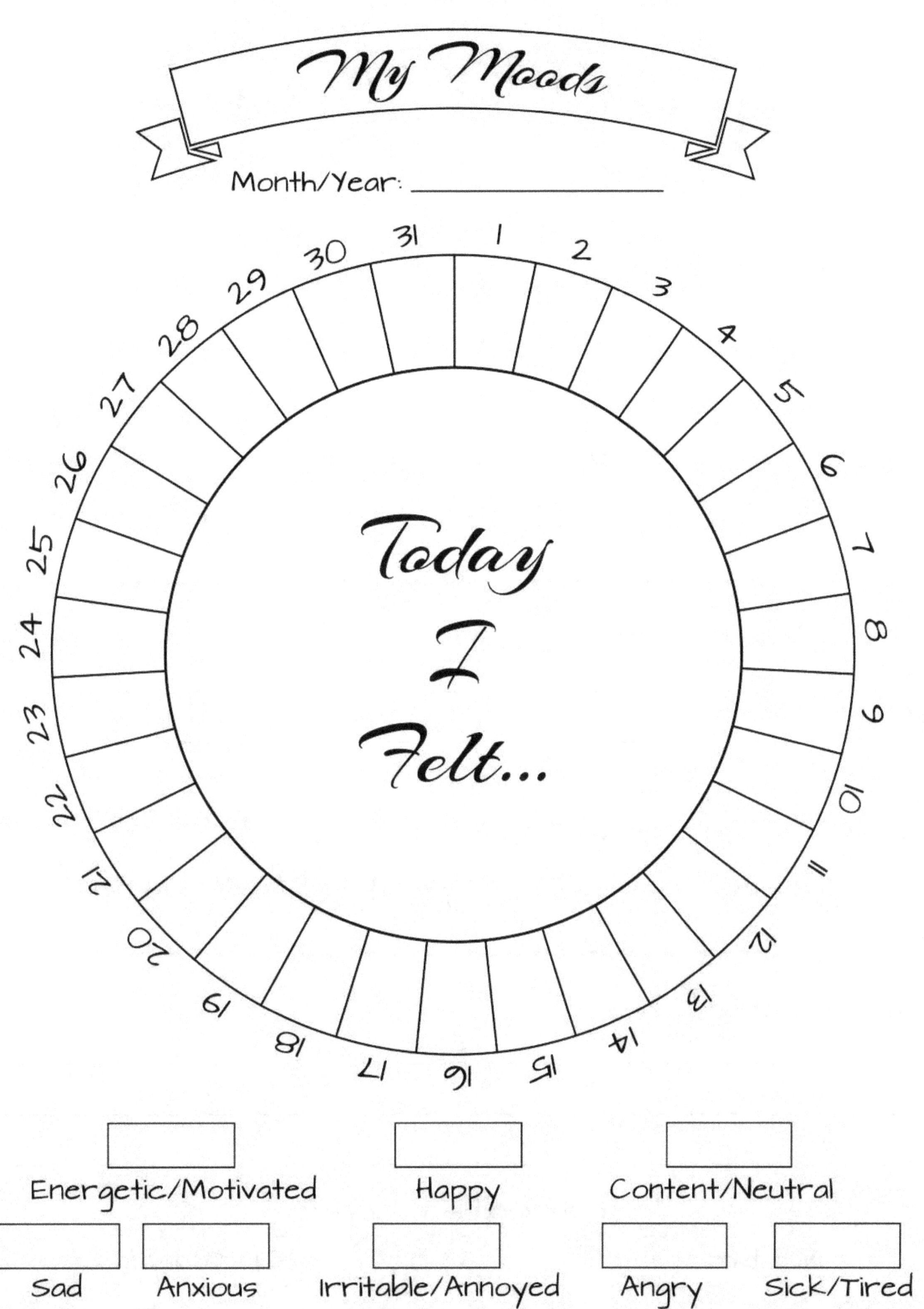

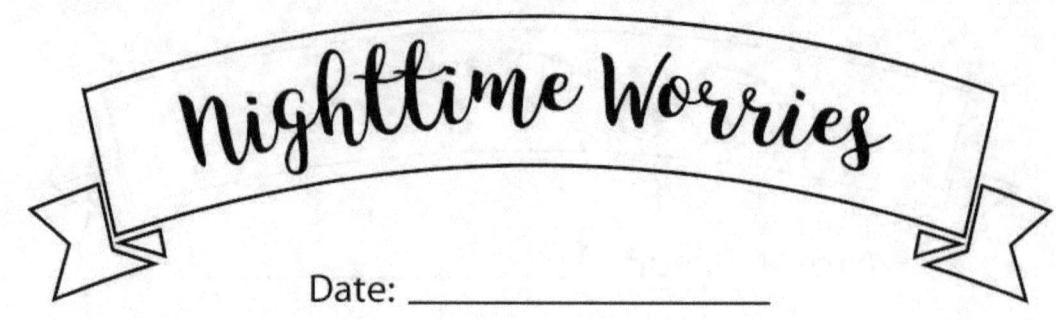

Nighttime Worries

Date: _____

I'm Worried About...

_____
_____
_____

How Bad is it Really?

Not Bad ① ② ③ ④ ⑤ Really Bad

I Feel Anxious About...

_____
_____
_____

How Bad is it Really?

Not Bad ① ② ③ ④ ⑤ Really Bad

I'm Concerned About...

_____
_____
_____

How Bad is it Really?

Not Bad ① ② ③ ④ ⑤ Really Bad

A Safe Space

Title of space _____

Sketch your safe space here

Words that describe your space

Sounds

Sights

Smells

Textures

People and animals present

A Safe Space

Title of space _____

Sketch your safe space here

Words that describe your space

Sounds

Sights

Smells

Textures

People and animals present

A Safe Space

Title of space _____

Sketch your safe space here

Words that describe your space

Sounds

Sights

Smells

Textures

People and animals present

A Safe Space

Title of space _____

Sketch your safe space here

Words that describe your space

Sounds

Sights

Smells

Textures

People and
animals present

A Safe Space

Title of space _____

Sketch your safe space here

Words that describe your space

Sounds

Sights

Smells

Textures

People and animals present

Body Scan

Today's Date _____   Time _____

Where are you? _____

Head and Face

Neck and Shoulders

Spine

Hips and Pelvis

Chest

Stomach

Arms

Legs

Whole body sensations

Sensations

Warm - Cold - Soft - Hard - Breeze - Damp - Dry
Tense - Strong - Taut - Numb - Tingling - Tickling - Muscle - Slender - Fragile
Pressure - Throbbing - Blocked - Pulse - Stabbing - Quivering
Nauseous - Shaking - Aching - Breathless - Wired - Anxious
Soothed - Relaxed - Comfortable - Free Flowing

Body Scan

Today's Date _____   Time _____

Where are you? _____

Head and Face

Neck and Shoulders

Spine

Hips and Pelvis

Chest

Stomach

Arms

Legs

Whole body sensations

Sensations

Warm - Cold - Soft - Hard - Breeze - Damp - Dry

Tense - Strong - Taut - Numb - Tingling - Tickling - Muscle - Slender - Fragile

Pressure - Throbbing - Blocked - Pulse - Stabbing - Quivering

Nauseous - Shaking - Aching - Breathless - Wired - Anxious

Soothed - Relaxed - Comfortable - Free Flowing

Body Scan

Today's Date _____   Time _____

Where are you? _____

Head and Face

Neck and Shoulders

Spine

Hips and Pelvis

Chest

Stomach

Arms

Legs

Whole body sensations

Sensations

Warm - Cold - Soft - Hard - Breeze - Damp - Dry

Tense - Strong - Taut - Numb - Tingling - Tickling - Muscle - Slender - Fragile

Pressure - Throbbing - Blocked - Pulse - Stabbing - Quivering

Nauseous - Shaking - Aching - Breathless - Wired - Anxious

Soothed - Relaxed - Comfortable - Free Flowing

Body Scan

Today's Date _____   Time _____

Where are you? _____

Head and Face

Neck and Shoulders

Spine

Hips and Pelvis

Chest

Stomach

Arms

Legs

Whole body sensations

Sensations

Warm - Cold - Soft - Hard - Breeze - Damp - Dry

Tense - Strong - Taut - Numb - Tingling - Tickling - Muscle - Slender - Fragile

Pressure - Throbbing - Blocked - Pulse - Stabbing - Quivering

Nauseous - Shaking - Aching - Breathless - Wired - Anxious

Soothed - Relaxed - Comfortable - Free Flowing

Body Scan

Today's Date _____   Time _____

Where are you? _____

Head and Face

Neck and Shoulders

Spine

Hips and Pelvis

Chest

Stomach

Arms

Legs

Whole body sensations

Sensations

Warm - Cold - Soft - Hard - Breeze - Damp - Dry
Tense - Strong - Taut - Numb - Tingling - Tickling - Muscle - Slender - Fragile
Pressure - Throbbing - Blocked - Pulse - Stabbing - Quivering
Nauseous - Shaking - Aching - Breathless - Wired - Anxious
Soothed - Relaxed - Comfortable - Free Flowing

Finger Labyrinth

Use your finger to slowly trace a path to the center of the labyrinth

Breathe calmly and slowly as you focus.
When you reach the center, draw a long deep breath or two.

Then trace your path back to the outside
Repeat until you feel more focused and calm.

Focus Words

Breathe - Peace - Relax - Tranquility - Serenity - Calm - Space - Beauty
Love - Wonder - Kindness - Light - Happiness - Joy - Warmth

Observations

Finger Labyrinth

Use your finger to slowly trace a path to the center of the labyrinth

Breathe calmly and slowly as you focus.
When you reach the center, draw a long deep breath or two.

Then trace your path back to the outside
Repeat until you feel more focused and calm.

Focus Words

Breathe - Peace - Relax - Tranquility - Serenity - Calm - Space - Beauty
Love - Wonder - Kindness - Light - Happiness - Joy - Warmth

Observations

Finger Labyrinth

Use your finger to slowly trace a path to the center of the labyrinth

Breathe calmly and slowly as you focus.
When you reach the center, draw a long deep breath or two.

Then trace your path back to the outside
Repeat until you feel more focused and calm.

Focus Words

Breathe - Peace - Relax - Tranquility - Serenity - Calm - Space - Beauty
Love - Wonder - Kindness - Light - Happiness - Joy - Warmth

Observations

Finger Labyrinth

Use your finger to slowly trace a path to the center of the labyrinth

Breathe calmly and slowly as you focus.
When you reach the center, draw a long deep breath or two.

Then trace your path back to the outside
Repeat until you feel more focused and calm.

Focus Words

Breathe - Peace - Relax - Tranquility - Serenity - Calm - Space - Beauty
Love - Wonder - Kindness - Light - Happiness - Joy - Warmth

Observations

Finger Labyrinth

Use your finger to slowly trace a path to the center of the labyrinth

Breathe calmly and slowly as you focus.
When you reach the center, draw a long deep breath or two.

Then trace your path back to the outside
Repeat until you feel more focused and calm.

Focus Words

Breathe - Peace - Relax - Tranquility - Serenity - Calm - Space - Beauty
Love - Wonder - Kindness - Light - Happiness - Joy - Warmth

Observations

Grounding Yourself

Today's Date _____

What is your name? _____

Where are you?

Words that describe your space

Who is with you? What are they doing?

Words that describe your feelings

What do you hear?

What do you see?

What can you smell?

What can you touch?

When you are calm, set an intention:

Grounding Yourself

Today's Date _____

What is your name? _____

Where are you?

Words that describe your space

Who is with you? What are they doing?

Words that describe your feelings

What do you hear?

What do you see?

What can you smell?

What can you touch?

When you are calm, set an intention:

Grounding Yourself

Today's Date _____

What is your name? _____

Where are you?

Words that describe your space

Who is with you? What are they doing?

Words that describe your feelings

What do you hear?

What do you see?

What can you smell?

What can you touch?

When you are calm, set an intention:

Grounding Yourself

Today's Date _____

What is your name? _____

Where are you?

Words that describe your space

Who is with you? What are they doing?

Words that describe your feelings

What do you hear?

What do you see?

What can you smell?

What can you touch?

When you are calm, set an intention:

Grounding Yourself

Today's Date _____

What is your name? _____

Where are you?

Words that describe your space

Who is with you? What are they doing?

Words that describe your feelings

What do you hear?

What do you see?

What can you smell?

What can you touch?

When you are calm, set an intention:

Happy Memory Clouds

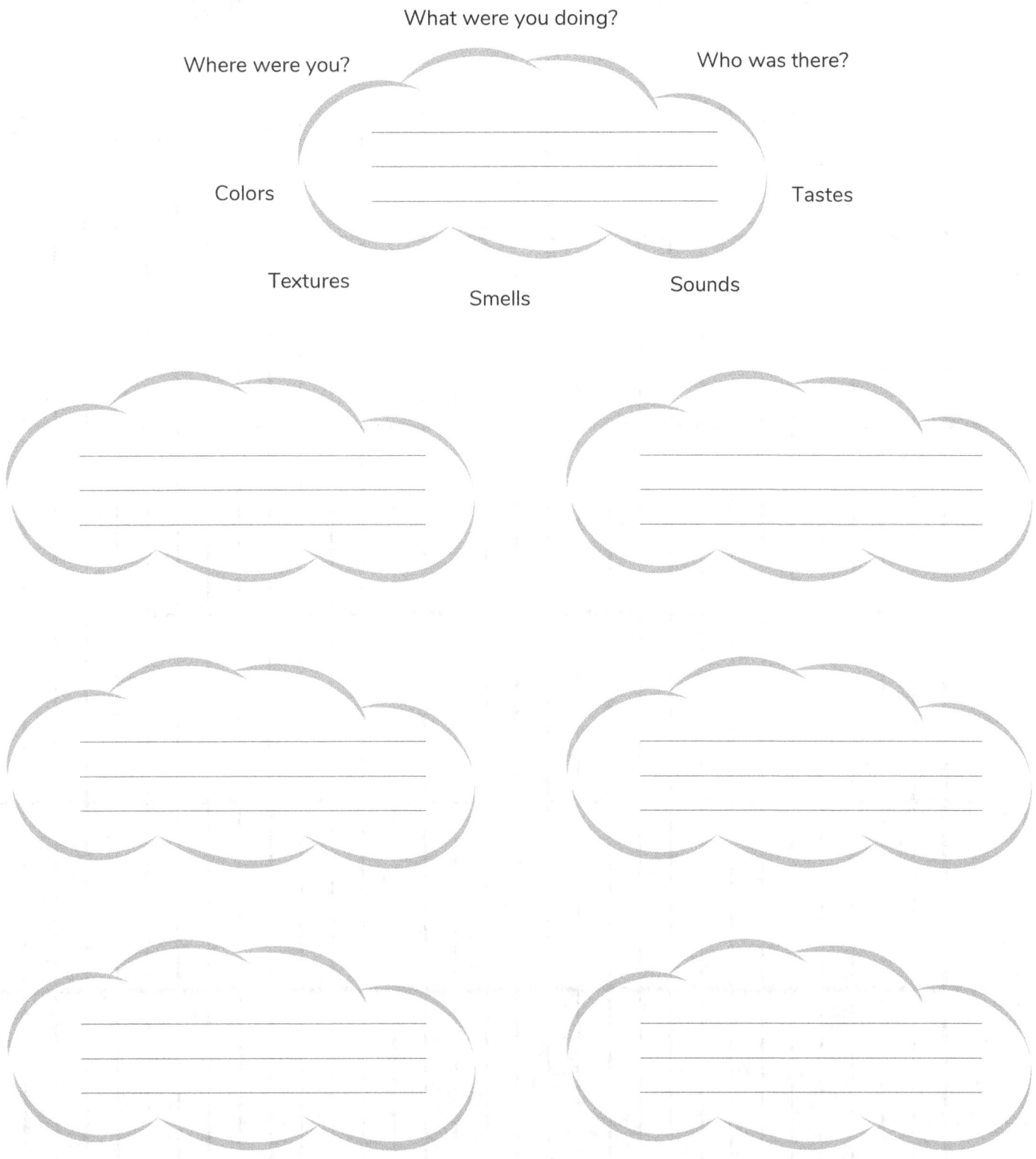

Fill out these clouds as you think of happy memories.
Use them when your emotions become overwhelming.

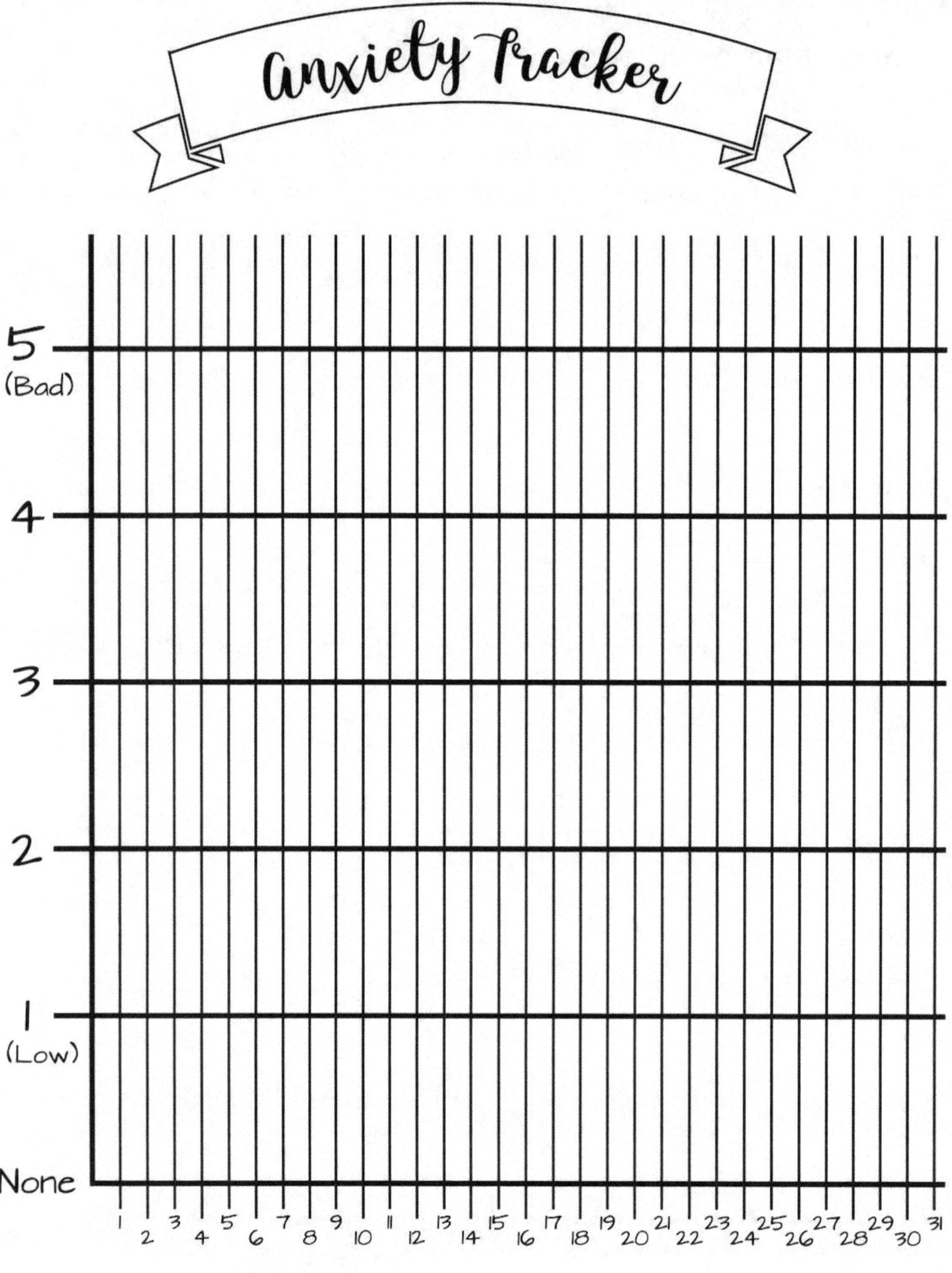

Date: _____

What Happened

_____
_____
_____

How I Reacted

_____
_____
_____

How Bad is it Really?	What I Think/Feel	How I'd Like to React Next Time
Not Bad		
①	_____	_____
②	_____	_____
③	_____	_____
④	_____	_____
⑤	_____	_____
Really Bad		

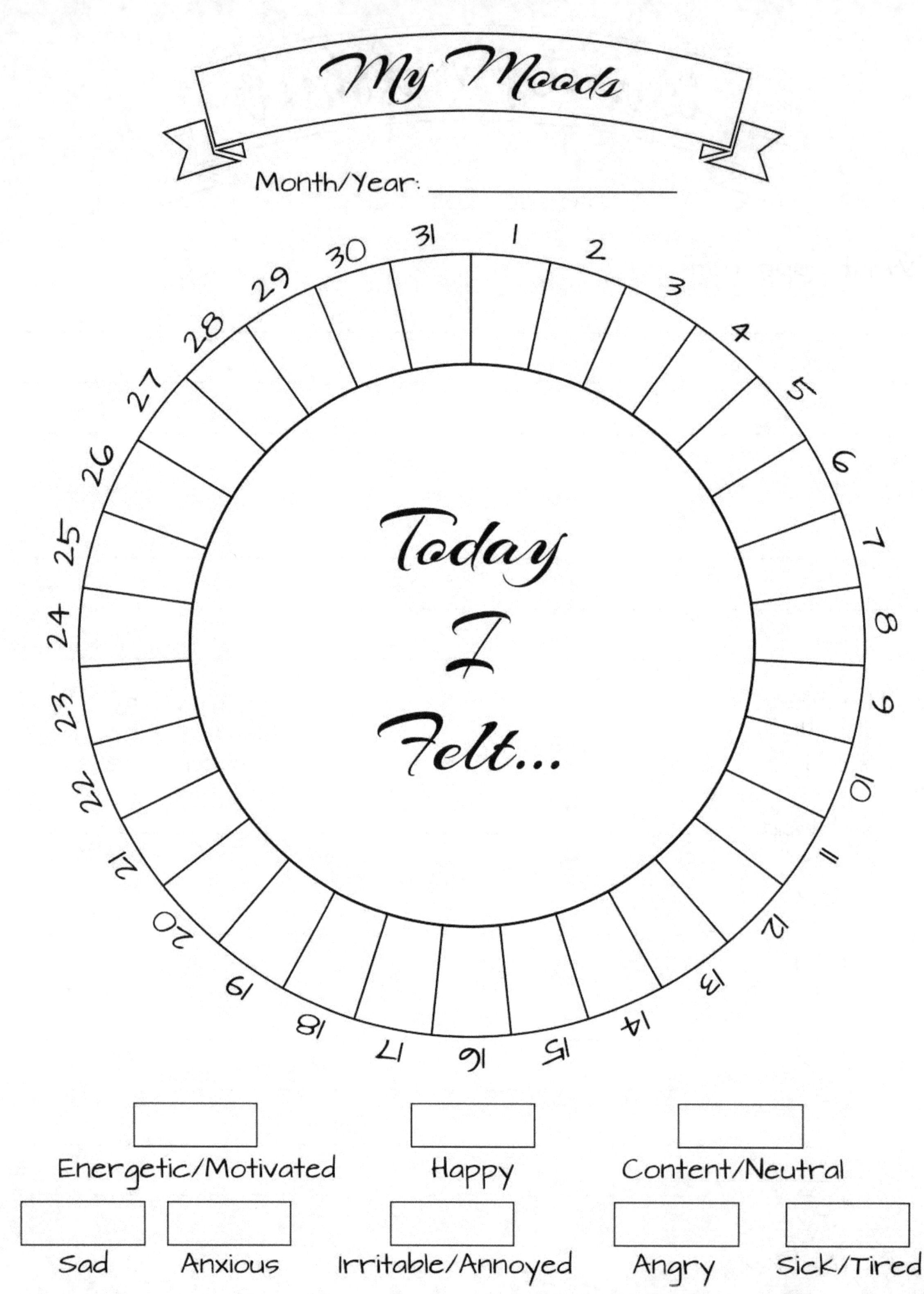

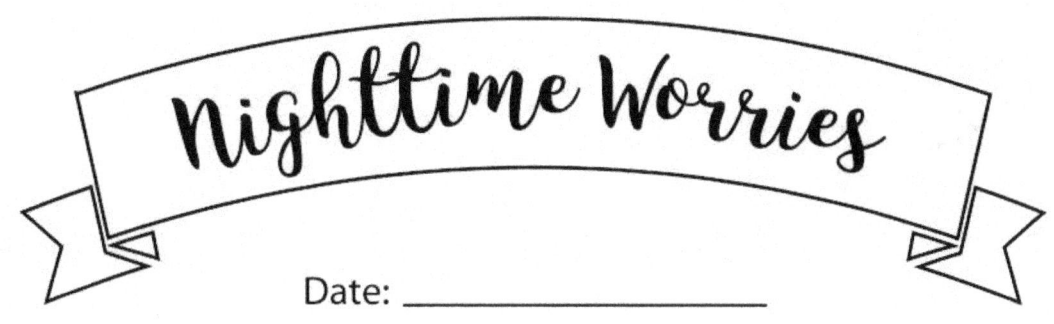

Date: _____

I'm Worried About...

_____
_____
_____

How Bad is it Really?

Not Bad ① ② ③ ④ ⑤ Really Bad

_____

I Feel Anxious About...

_____
_____
_____

How Bad is it Really?

Not Bad ① ② ③ ④ ⑤ Really Bad

_____

I'm Concerned About...

_____
_____
_____

How Bad is it Really?

Not Bad ① ② ③ ④ ⑤ Really Bad

A Safe Space

Title of space _____

Sketch your safe space here

Words that describe your space

Sounds

Sights

Smells

Textures

People and animals present

A Safe Space

Title of space _____

Sketch your safe space here

Words that describe your space

Sounds

Sights

Smells

Textures

People and animals present

A Safe Space

Title of space _____

Sketch your safe space here

Words that describe your space

Sounds

Sights

Smells

Textures

People and animals present

A Safe Space

Title of space _____

Sketch your safe space here

Words that describe your space

Sounds

Sights

Smells

Textures

People and animals present

A Safe Space

Title of space _____

Sketch your safe space here

Words that describe your space

Sounds

Sights

Smells

Textures

People and animals present

Body Scan

Today's Date _____   Time _____

Where are you? _____

Head and Face

Neck and Shoulders

Spine

Hips and Pelvis

Chest

Stomach

Arms

Legs

Whole body sensations

Sensations

Warm - Cold - Soft - Hard - Breeze - Damp - Dry

Tense - Strong - Taut - Numb - Tingling - Tickling - Muscle - Slender - Fragile

Pressure - Throbbing - Blocked - Pulse - Stabbing - Quivering

Nauseous - Shaking - Aching - Breathless - Wired - Anxious

Soothed - Relaxed - Comfortable - Free Flowing

Body Scan

Today's Date _____   Time _____

Where are you? _____

Head and Face

Chest

Neck and Shoulders

Stomach

Spine

Arms

Hips and Pelvis

Legs

Whole body sensations

Sensations

Warm - Cold - Soft - Hard - Breeze - Damp - Dry

Tense - Strong - Taut - Numb - Tingling - Tickling - Muscle - Slender - Fragile

Pressure - Throbbing - Blocked - Pulse - Stabbing - Quivering

Nauseous - Shaking - Aching - Breathless - Wired - Anxious

Soothed - Relaxed - Comfortable - Free Flowing

Body Scan

Today's Date _____   Time _____

Where are you? _____

Head and Face

Neck and Shoulders

Spine

Hips and Pelvis

Chest

Stomach

Arms

Legs

Whole body sensations

Sensations

Warm - Cold - Soft - Hard - Breeze - Damp - Dry

Tense - Strong - Taut - Numb - Tingling - Tickling - Muscle - Slender - Fragile

Pressure - Throbbing - Blocked - Pulse - Stabbing - Quivering

Nauseous - Shaking - Aching - Breathless - Wired - Anxious

Soothed - Relaxed - Comfortable - Free Flowing

Body Scan

Today's Date _____ Time _____

Where are you? _____

Head and Face

Neck and Shoulders

Spine

Hips and Pelvis

Chest

Stomach

Arms

Legs

Whole body sensations

Sensations

Warm - Cold - Soft - Hard - Breeze - Damp - Dry

Tense - Strong - Taut - Numb - Tingling - Tickling - Muscle - Slender - Fragile

Pressure - Throbbing - Blocked - Pulse - Stabbing - Quivering

Nauseous - Shaking - Aching - Breathless - Wired - Anxious

Soothed - Relaxed - Comfortable - Free Flowing

Body Scan

Today's Date _____   Time _____

Where are you? _____

Head and Face

Neck and Shoulders

Spine

Hips and Pelvis

Chest

Stomach

Arms

Legs

Whole body sensations

Sensations

Warm - Cold - Soft - Hard - Breeze - Damp - Dry

Tense - Strong - Taut - Numb - Tingling - Tickling - Muscle - Slender - Fragile

Pressure - Throbbing - Blocked - Pulse - Stabbing - Quivering

Nauseous - Shaking - Aching - Breathless - Wired - Anxious

Soothed - Relaxed - Comfortable - Free Flowing

Finger Labyrinth

Use your finger to slowly trace a path to the center of the labyrinth

Breathe calmly and slowly as you focus.
When you reach the center, draw a long deep breath or two.

Then trace your path back to the outside
Repeat until you feel more focused and calm.

Focus Words

Breathe - Peace - Relax - Tranquility - Serenity - Calm - Space - Beauty
Love - Wonder - Kindness - Light - Happiness - Joy - Warmth

Observations

Finger Labyrinth

Use your finger to slowly trace a path to the center of the labyrinth

Breathe calmly and slowly as you focus.
When you reach the center, draw a long deep breath or two.

Then trace your path back to the outside
Repeat until you feel more focused and calm.

Focus Words

Breathe - Peace - Relax - Tranquility - Serenity - Calm - Space - Beauty
Love - Wonder - Kindness - Light - Happiness - Joy - Warmth

Observations

Finger Labyrinth

Use your finger to slowly trace a path to the center of the labyrinth

Breathe calmly and slowly as you focus.
When you reach the center, draw a long deep breath or two.

Then trace your path back to the outside
Repeat until you feel more focused and calm.

Focus Words

Breathe - Peace - Relax - Tranquility - Serenity - Calm - Space - Beauty
Love - Wonder - Kindness - Light - Happiness - Joy - Warmth

Observations

Finger Labyrinth

Use your finger to slowly trace a path to the center of the labyrinth

Breathe calmly and slowly as you focus.
When you reach the center, draw a long deep breath or two.

Then trace your path back to the outside
Repeat until you feel more focused and calm.

Focus Words

Breathe - Peace - Relax - Tranquility - Serenity - Calm - Space - Beauty
Love - Wonder - Kindness - Light - Happiness - Joy - Warmth

Observations

Finger Labyrinth

Use your finger to slowly trace a path to the center of the labyrinth

Breathe calmly and slowly as you focus.
When you reach the center, draw a long deep breath or two.

Then trace your path back to the outside
Repeat until you feel more focused and calm.

Focus Words

Breathe - Peace - Relax - Tranquility - Serenity - Calm - Space - Beauty
Love - Wonder - Kindness - Light - Happiness - Joy - Warmth

Observations

Grounding Yourself

Today's Date _____

What is your name? _____

Where are you?

Words that describe your space

Who is with you? What are they doing?

Words that describe your feelings

What do you hear?

What do you see?

What can you smell?

What can you touch?

When you are calm, set an intention:

Grounding Yourself

Today's Date _____

What is your name? _____

Where are you?

Words that describe your space

Who is with you? What are they doing?

Words that describe your feelings

What do you hear?

What do you see?

What can you smell?

What can you touch?

When you are calm, set an intention:

Grounding Yourself

Today's Date _____

What is your name? _____

Where are you?

Words that describe your space

Who is with you? What are they doing?

Words that describe your feelings

What do you hear?

What do you see?

What can you smell?

What can you touch?

When you are calm, set an intention:

Grounding Yourself

Today's Date _____

What is your name? _____

Where are you?

Words that describe your space

Who is with you? What are they doing?

Words that describe your feelings

What do you hear?

What do you see?

What can you smell?

What can you touch?

When you are calm, set an intention:

Grounding Yourself

Today's Date _____

What is your name? _____

Where are you?

Words that describe your space

Who is with you? What are they doing?

Words that describe your feelings

What do you hear?

What do you see?

What can you smell?

What can you touch?

When you are calm, set an intention:

Happy Memory Clouds

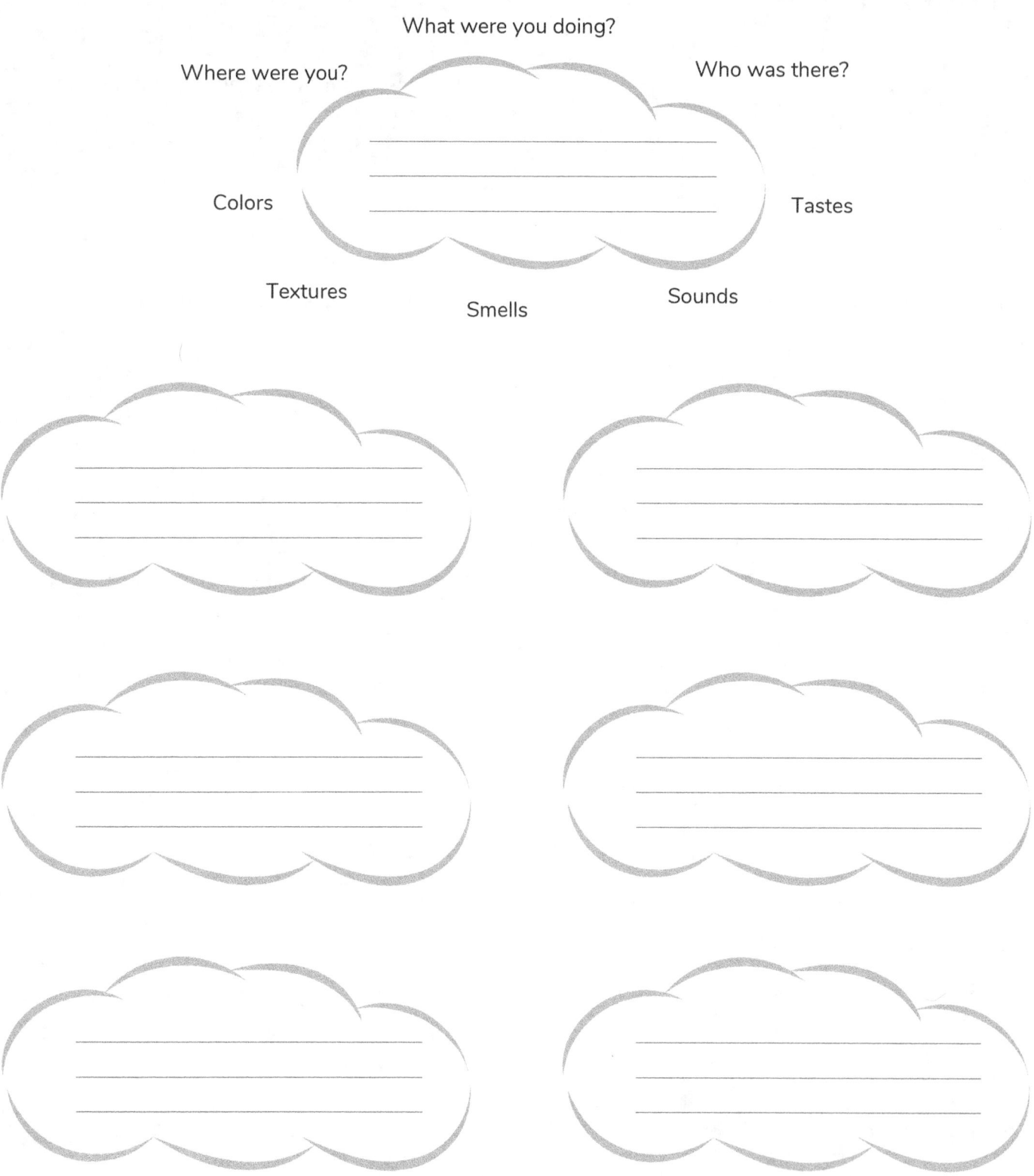

What were you doing?
Where were you?   Who was there?
Colors   Tastes
Textures   Sounds
Smells

Fill out these clouds as you think of happy memories.
Use them when your emotions become overwhelming.

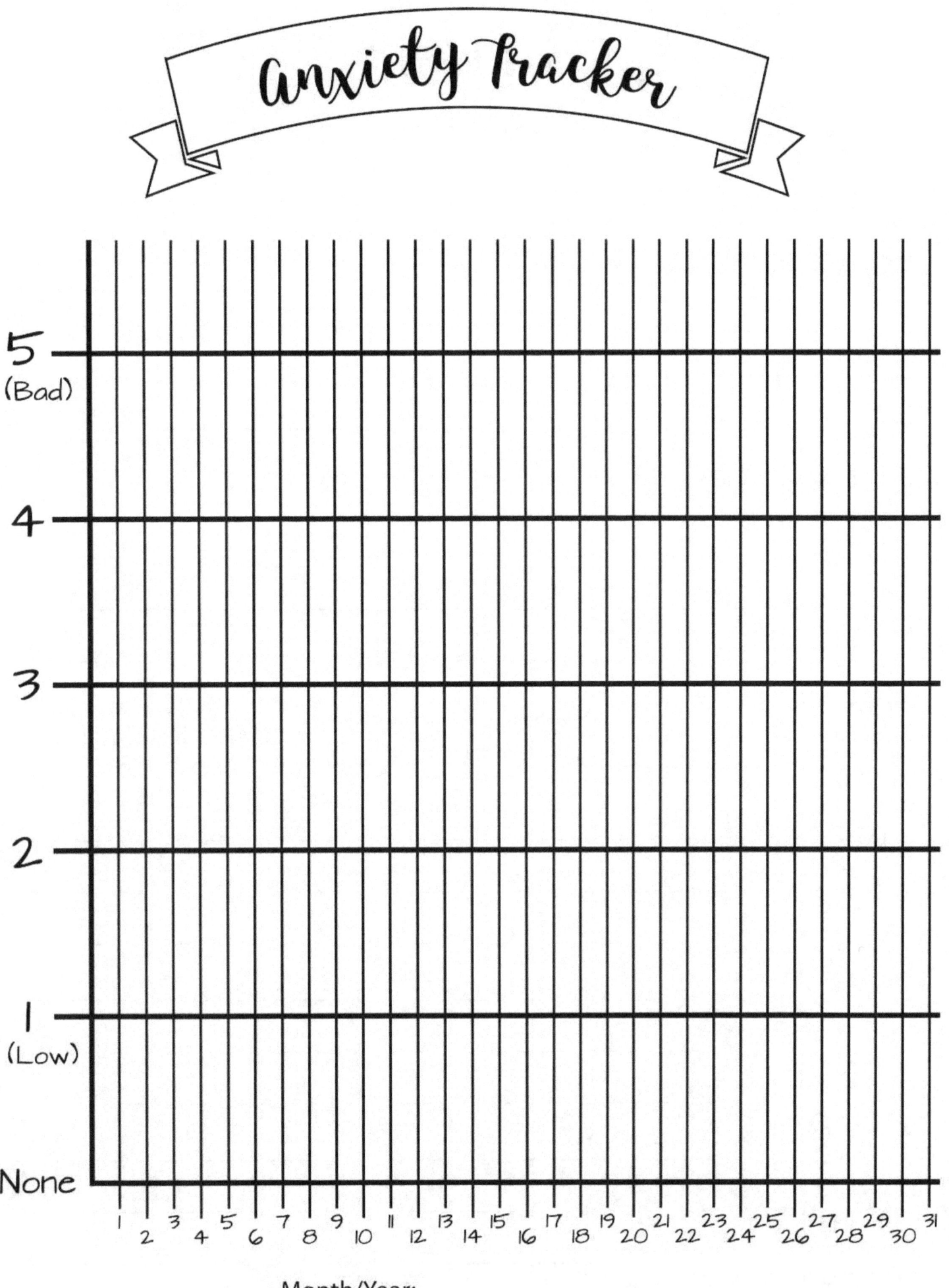

Anxiety Worksheet

Date: _____

What Happened

_____
_____
_____

How I Reacted

_____
_____
_____

How Bad is it Really?	What I Think/Feel	How I'd Like to React Next Time
Not Bad		
①	_____	_____
②	_____	_____
③	_____	_____
④	_____	_____
⑤	_____	_____
Really Bad		

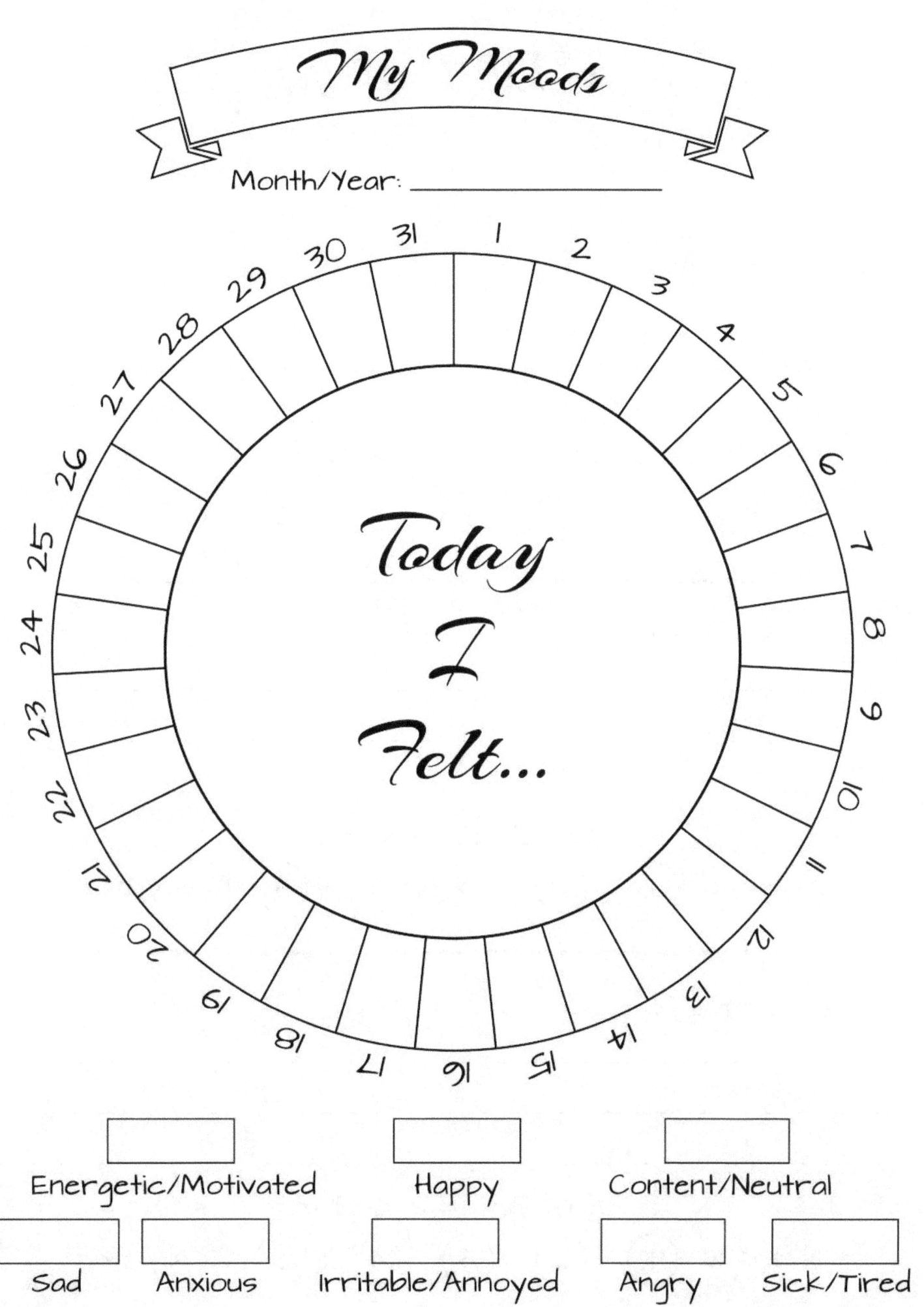

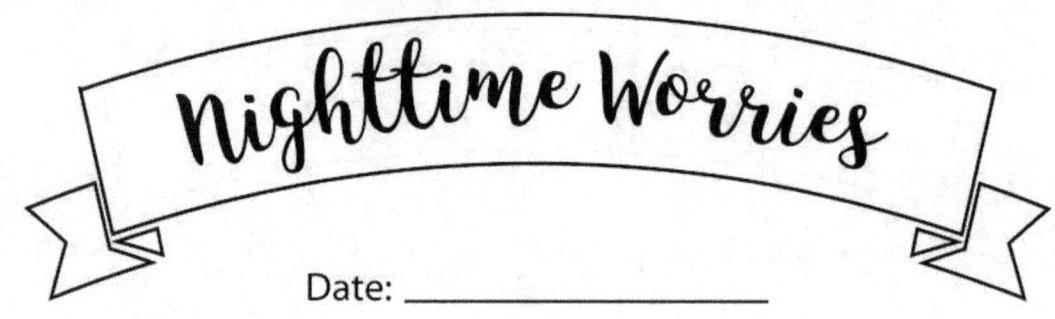

Nighttime Worries

Date: _____

I'm Worried About...

_____
_____
_____

How Bad is it Really?

Not Bad ① ② ③ ④ ⑤ Really Bad

I Feel Anxious About...

_____
_____
_____

How Bad is it Really?

Not Bad ① ② ③ ④ ⑤ Really Bad

I'm Concerned About...

_____
_____
_____

How Bad is it Really?

Not Bad ① ② ③ ④ ⑤ Really Bad

A Safe Space

Title of space _____

Sketch your safe space here

Words that describe your space

Sounds

Sights

Smells

Textures

People and animals present

A Safe Space

Title of space _____

Sketch your safe space here

Words that describe your space

Sounds

Sights

Smells

Textures

People and animals present

A Safe Space

Title of space _____

Sketch your safe space here

Words that describe your space

Sounds

Sights

Smells

Textures

People and animals present

A Safe Space

Title of space _____

Sketch your safe space here

Words that describe your space

Sounds

Sights

Smells

Textures

People and
animals present

A Safe Space

Title of space _____

Sketch your safe space here

Words that describe your space

Sounds

Sights

Smells

Textures

People and animals present

Body Scan

Today's Date _____   Time _____

Where are you? _____

Head and Face

Neck and Shoulders

Spine

Hips and Pelvis

Chest

Stomach

Arms

Legs

Whole body sensations

Sensations

Warm - Cold - Soft - Hard - Breeze - Damp - Dry

Tense - Strong - Taut - Numb - Tingling - Tickling - Muscle - Slender - Fragile

Pressure - Throbbing - Blocked - Pulse - Stabbing - Quivering

Nauseous - Shaking - Aching - Breathless - Wired - Anxious

Soothed - Relaxed - Comfortable - Free Flowing

Body Scan

Today's Date _____   Time _____

Where are you? _____

Head and Face

Neck and Shoulders

Spine

Hips and Pelvis

Chest

Stomach

Arms

Legs

Whole body sensations

Sensations

Warm - Cold - Soft - Hard - Breeze - Damp - Dry

Tense - Strong - Taut - Numb - Tingling - Tickling - Muscle - Slender - Fragile

Pressure - Throbbing - Blocked - Pulse - Stabbing - Quivering

Nauseous - Shaking - Aching - Breathless - Wired - Anxious

Soothed - Relaxed - Comfortable - Free Flowing

Body Scan

Today's Date _____   Time _____

Where are you? _____

Head and Face

Neck and Shoulders

Spine

Hips and Pelvis

Chest

Stomach

Arms

Legs

Whole body sensations

Sensations

Warm - Cold - Soft - Hard - Breeze - Damp - Dry

Tense - Strong - Taut - Numb - Tingling - Tickling - Muscle - Slender - Fragile

Pressure - Throbbing - Blocked - Pulse - Stabbing - Quivering

Nauseous - Shaking - Aching - Breathless - Wired - Anxious

Soothed - Relaxed - Comfortable - Free Flowing

Body Scan

Today's Date _____   Time _____

Where are you? _____

Head and Face

Neck and Shoulders

Spine

Hips and Pelvis

Chest

Stomach

Arms

Legs

Whole body sensations

Sensations

Warm - Cold - Soft - Hard - Breeze - Damp - Dry
Tense - Strong - Taut - Numb - Tingling - Tickling - Muscle - Slender - Fragile
Pressure - Throbbing - Blocked - Pulse - Stabbing - Quivering
Nauseous - Shaking - Aching - Breathless - Wired - Anxious
Soothed - Relaxed - Comfortable - Free Flowing

Body Scan

Today's Date _____   Time _____

Where are you? _____

Head and Face

Neck and Shoulders

Spine

Hips and Pelvis

Chest

Stomach

Arms

Legs

Whole body sensations

Sensations

Warm - Cold - Soft - Hard - Breeze - Damp - Dry

Tense - Strong - Taut - Numb - Tingling - Tickling - Muscle - Slender - Fragile

Pressure - Throbbing - Blocked - Pulse - Stabbing - Quivering

Nauseous - Shaking - Aching - Breathless - Wired - Anxious

Soothed - Relaxed - Comfortable - Free Flowing

Finger Labyrinth

Use your finger to slowly trace a path to the center of the labyrinth

Breathe calmly and slowly as you focus.
When you reach the center, draw a long deep breath or two.

Then trace your path back to the outside
Repeat until you feel more focused and calm.

Focus Words

Breathe - Peace - Relax - Tranquility - Serenity - Calm - Space - Beauty
Love - Wonder - Kindness - Light - Happiness - Joy - Warmth

Observations

Finger Labyrinth

Use your finger to slowly trace a path to the center of the labyrinth

Breathe calmly and slowly as you focus.
When you reach the center, draw a long deep breath or two.

Then trace your path back to the outside
Repeat until you feel more focused and calm.

Focus Words

Breathe - Peace - Relax - Tranquility - Serenity - Calm - Space - Beauty
Love - Wonder - Kindness - Light - Happiness - Joy - Warmth

Observations

Finger Labyrinth

Use your finger to slowly trace a path to the center of the labyrinth

Breathe calmly and slowly as you focus.
When you reach the center, draw a long deep breath or two.

Then trace your path back to the outside
Repeat until you feel more focused and calm.

Focus Words

Breathe - Peace - Relax - Tranquility - Serenity - Calm - Space - Beauty
Love - Wonder - Kindness - Light - Happiness - Joy - Warmth

Observations

Finger Labyrinth

Use your finger to slowly trace a path to the center of the labyrinth

Breathe calmly and slowly as you focus.
When you reach the center, draw a long deep breath or two.

Then trace your path back to the outside
Repeat until you feel more focused and calm.

Focus Words

Breathe - Peace - Relax - Tranquility - Serenity - Calm - Space - Beauty
Love - Wonder - Kindness - Light - Happiness - Joy - Warmth

Observations

Finger Labyrinth

Use your finger to slowly trace a path to the center of the labyrinth

Breathe calmly and slowly as you focus.
When you reach the center, draw a long deep breath or two.

Then trace your path back to the outside
Repeat until you feel more focused and calm.

Focus Words

Breathe - Peace - Relax - Tranquility - Serenity - Calm - Space - Beauty
Love - Wonder - Kindness - Light - Happiness - Joy - Warmth

Observations

Grounding Yourself

Today's Date _____

What is your name? _____

Where are you?

Words that describe your space

Who is with you? What are they doing?

Words that describe your feelings

What do you hear?

What do you see?

What can you smell?

What can you touch?

When you are calm, set an intention:

Grounding Yourself

Today's Date _____

What is your name? _____

Where are you?

Words that describe your space

Who is with you? What are they doing?

Words that describe your feelings

What do you hear?

What do you see?

What can you smell?

What can you touch?

When you are calm, set an intention:

Grounding Yourself

Today's Date _____

What is your name? _____

Where are you?

Words that describe your space

Who is with you? What are they doing?

Words that describe your feelings

What do you hear?

What do you see?

What can you smell?

What can you touch?

When you are calm, set an intention:

Grounding Yourself

Today's Date _____

What is your name? _____

Where are you?

Words that describe your space

Who is with you? What are they doing?

Words that describe your feelings

What do you hear?

What do you see?

What can you smell?

What can you touch?

When you are calm, set an intention:

Grounding Yourself

Today's Date _____

What is your name? _____

Where are you?

Words that describe your space

Who is with you? What are they doing?

Words that describe your feelings

What do you hear?

What do you see?

What can you smell?

What can you touch?

When you are calm, set an intention:

Happy Memory Clouds

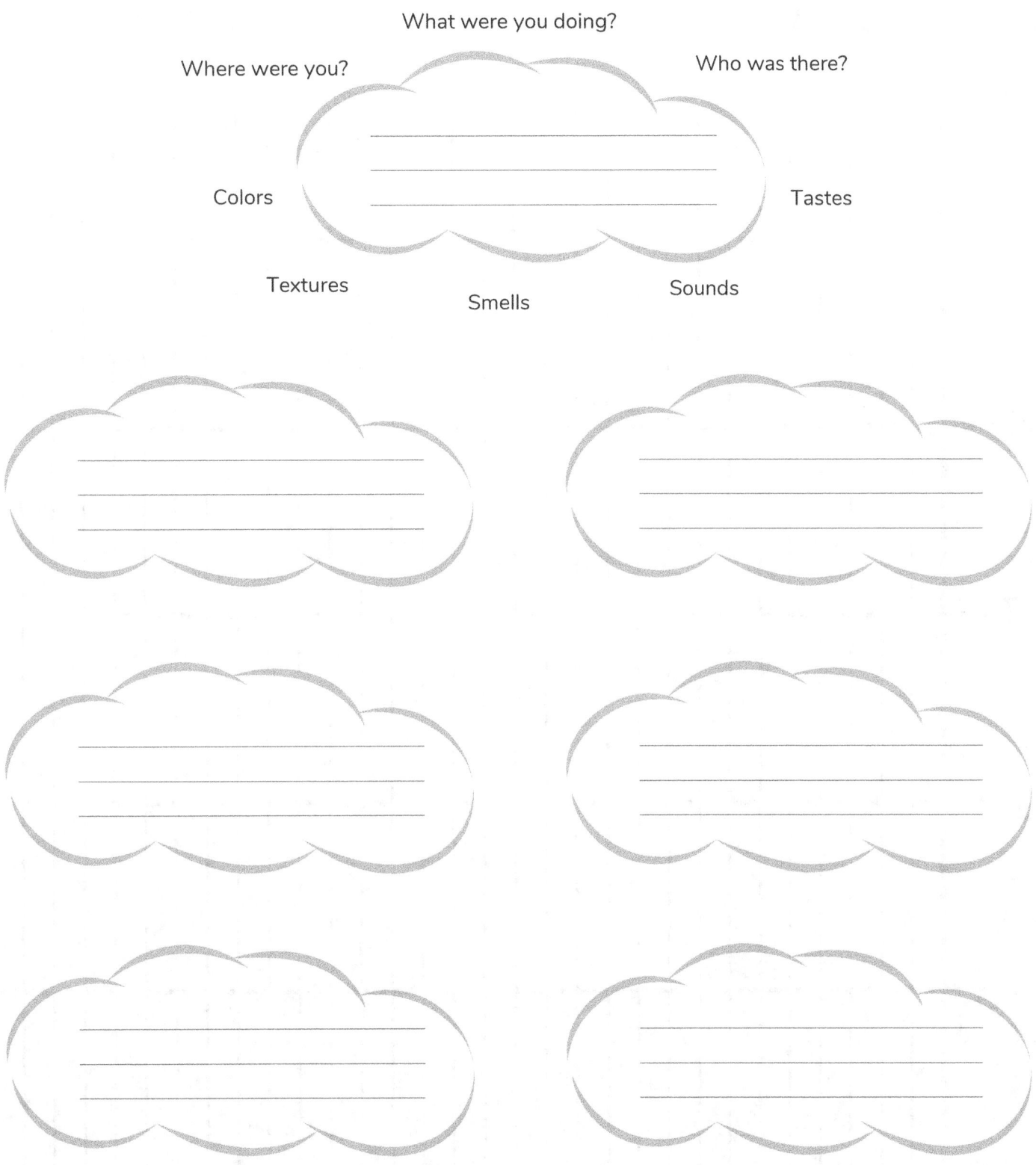

Fill out these clouds as you think of happy memories.
Use them when your emotions become overwhelming.

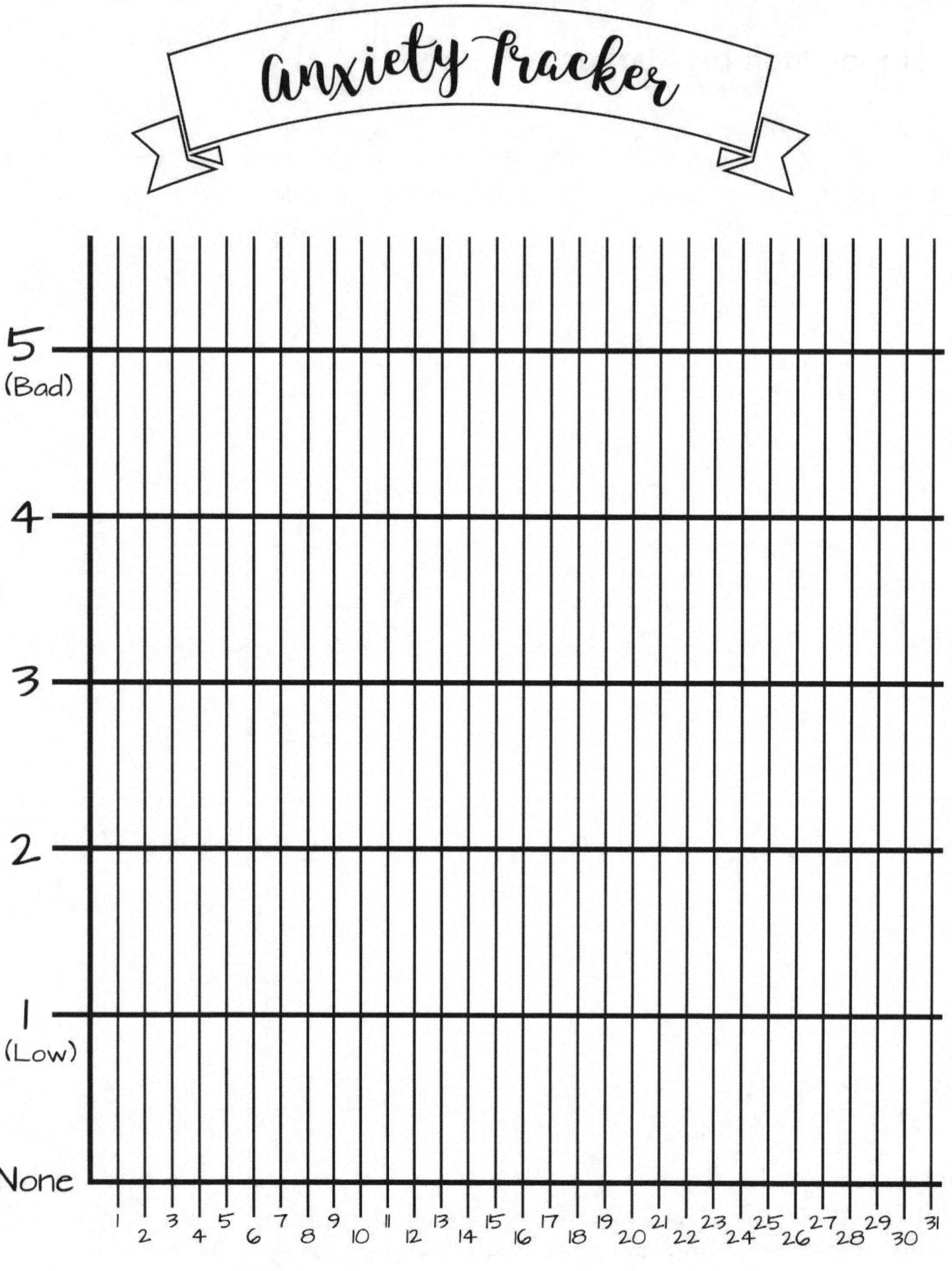

Anxiety Worksheet

Date: _____

What Happened

_____
_____
_____

How I Reacted

_____
_____
_____

How Bad is it Really?	What I Think/Feel	How I'd Like to React Next Time
Not Bad	_____	_____
①	_____	_____
	_____	_____
②	_____	_____
	_____	_____
③	_____	_____
	_____	_____
④	_____	_____
	_____	_____
⑤	_____	_____
Really Bad		

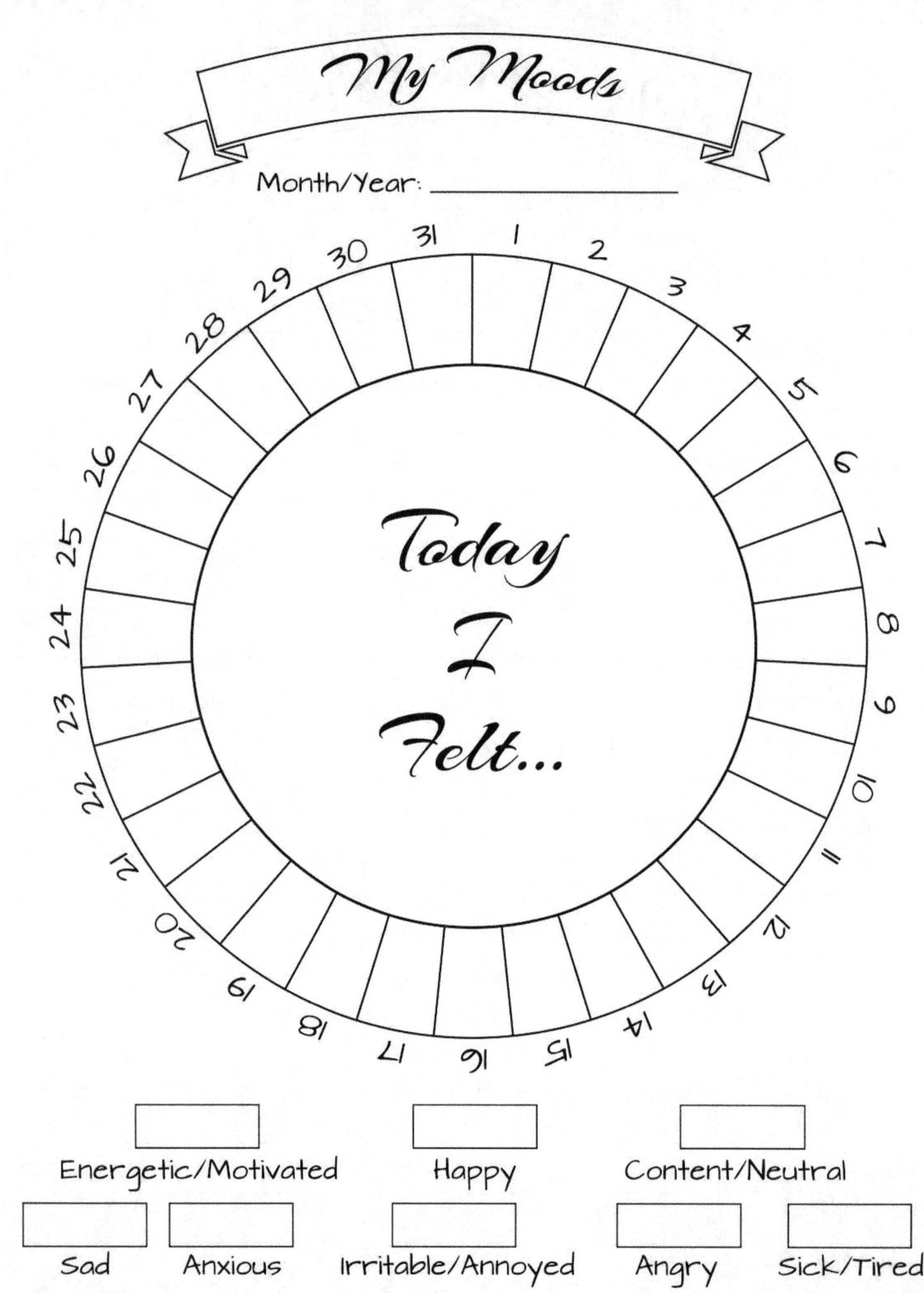

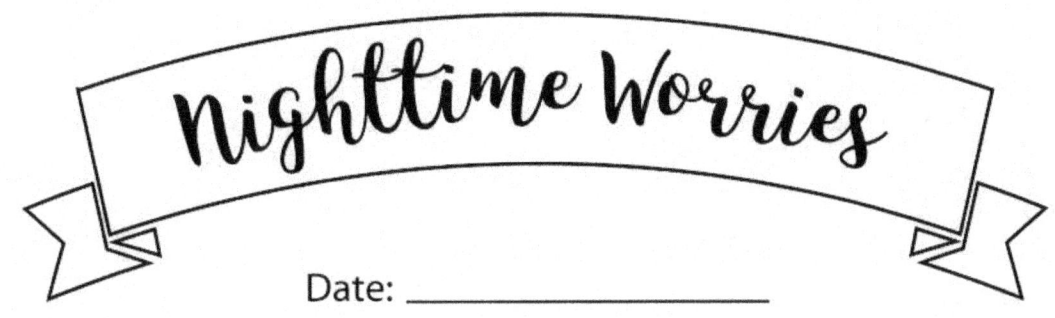

Date: _____

I'm Worried About...

_____
_____
_____

How Bad is it Really?

Not Bad ① ② ③ ④ ⑤ Really Bad

_____

I Feel Anxious About...

_____
_____
_____

How Bad is it Really?

Not Bad ① ② ③ ④ ⑤ Really Bad

_____

I'm Concerned About...

_____
_____
_____

How Bad is it Really?

Not Bad ① ② ③ ④ ⑤ Really Bad

A Safe Space

Title of space _____

Sketch your safe space here

Words that describe your space

Sounds

Sights

Smells

Textures

People and animals present

A Safe Space

Title of space _____

Sketch your safe space here

Words that describe your space

Sounds

Sights

Smells

Textures

People and animals present

A Safe Space

Title of space _____

Sketch your safe space here

Words that describe your space

Sounds

Sights

Smells

Textures

People and animals present

A Safe Space

Title of space _____

Sketch your safe space here

Words that describe your space

Sounds

Sights

Smells

Textures

People and animals present

A Safe Space

Title of space _____

Sketch your safe space here

Words that describe your space

Sounds

Sights

Smells

Textures

People and animals present

A Safe Space

Title of space _____

Sketch your safe space here

Words that describe your space

Sounds

Sights

Smells

Textures

People and animals present

A Safe Space

Title of space _____

Sketch your safe space here

Words that describe your space

Sounds

Sights

Smells

Textures

People and animals present

www.ingramcontent.com/pod-product-compliance
Lightning Source LLC
Chambersburg PA
CBHW081156070526
44583CB00021B/2860